Self-Mocking Humour

and a
Bellyful of Cider

By

Ian Shipley

Grosvenor House
Publishing Limited

This book is published by
Grosvenor House Publishing Ltd
Link House
140 The Broadway, Tolworth, Surrey, KT6 7HT.
www.grosvenorhousepublishing.co.uk

A CIP record for this book
is available from the British Library

ISBN 978-1-80381-148-2

Dedication

Alison Louise Shipley-Whitehead
1970 – 2019
Aged 48

Love and Laughs Forever

Contents

CHAPTER 1

The Best Things in Life Are Silly

The Demon Dentist

I broke a tooth on Saturday night
Now it's like a razor-sharp dagger
So I've got to go and get it sorted
Before it turns into an infected throbber
It's annoying and uncomfortable
And it's lacerating my tongue
So on Monday I booked an appointment
Though I'm not keen to go along

To see the demon dentist
The Nottinghamshire driller-killer
But it's time to man up I'm afraid
And face the dental fiend
With his pliers and filler

It won't be a joyous occasion
Lying in his chair
Staring at the ceiling
Feeling anguish and despair
Cos I've had this tooth for over fifty years
It hasn't half served me well
When I think of all the food it's chewed
Thank you, upper left six, and farewell

"Open wide and relax," he said
That's easy for him to say
Then he stabbed me in the roof of my mouth
And twice more in the gum
"We'll have that one out, and that one filled," he said,
"Now, are we ready? Is it numb?"

He pulled and tugged then I heard a crack
He wiggled it about
And with one last jerk out it came
He'd freed it from my mouth
"One cracked molar now extracted," he joyfully declared,
"Now I'll do the filling"
But by that point, I no longer cared

They say, "There's no pain like tooth pain"
But the pain was in my wallet
Waiting at reception was my itemised bill
I couldn't believe what was on it
Nearly four hundred pounds
I wasn't expecting that
"I'll see you again in six months," he said
I smiled and thought, *Yeah, sod that*

It's Just a Bit of Man Flu

Lying there festering in my bed
I think I've got Ebola
My wife she laughs, says, "Don't be daft
It's just a bit of man flu"
But I've been sneezing mucus
It's hanging from my nose
I don't need to see a doctor
'Cause my wife she says she knows
It's just a bit of man flu
It'll be gone in a couple of days
But I don't believe I'll live that long
So I think I'll write my will

My throat it feels like sandpaper
I've overdosed on Lemsip
My wife she jokes, says, "You won't croak
It's just a bit of man flu"
But what if it's pneumonia?
What about my chesty cough?
I'm feeling quite congested
My sinuses are blocked
But it's just a bit of man flu
'Cause my wife, she diagnosed
So all I need is two days' rest
To clear this stinking cold

The following week and I'm in trouble
For passing on my germs
I said, "I'm sorry, wife, but it's fair to share,
Besides, it's just a bit of man flu"
She tried to be a martyr
And carry on regardless
But when she looked like death warmed up
She soon put on her pyjamas
Sprawled out on the sofa
She was not impressed
Especially when I volunteered
To rub ointment on her chest

It might just be an old wives' tale
But when you've got the flu
Don't let it put you in your grave
This is what you do
Help fight the winter sniffles
When you're feeling under the weather
Warm up a bowl of chicken soup
And suddenly, you'll feel, much, much better

Mouldy Sandwich

It was time to take a well-earned break
It was lunchtime, one o'clock
The wife had packed me some sarnies
I couldn't wait to see what I'd got
Ham, cheese and pickle
Very, very nice
My taste buds were tingling
With pure delight

Starving I was
But something smelt wrong
My lunchtime snack had a potent pong
Yes, my butty smelt funny
Like a festering cabbage
It wasn't my banana
Or my home-grown radish

Well, I grabbed my sarnie
I took a massive big bite
It was then I noticed fuzzy bits
Were growing on the side
It was green on the bottom
Blue around the edge
Cultivating nicely, growing on my bread
Penicillin, on my wholemeal loaf
I thought, *I'm still going to eat it*
'Cause I've got nowt else

I glared at my butty
But I was famished
I thought, *The wife's trying to kill me*
With a mouldy old sandwich
I couldn't bear to bin it
So I tore off the crust
Scraped off the fungus
And ate what I could

Despite the wife's attempt on my life
With an out-of-date bread loaf
I felt alright
No, it did me no harm
Ingesting some mould
'Cause for the past few years
I haven't had a cold

Wellingtons

When your sock falls down in your wellington
When it's neither on nor off
When it disappears inside your boot
It don't half hack you off
Yes, it really is annoying
When your sock's hanging off your toes
And the snow is deep and the mud is thick
And your feet are blue with cold

When your sock falls down in your wellington
And you're trying to pull it up
Then your boot it springs a leak
And now you've one wet foot
A floppy sock it is no good
Squelching when you stroll
And your poor old toes have shrivelled up
And your feet look really old

When your sock falls down in your wellington
And you're hopping around like a frog
Out of breath, I must confess,
I hate my welly-gogz
Left on right, right on left
It's easy to mix them up
They're clumsy and uncomfortable
And I have had enough

When your sock falls down in your wellington
And it fills you with despair
It's time to buy some sturdy boots
Like proper walkers wear
I think I've learnt my lesson
I should never have put them on
So I've chucked them in the outside shed
Because that's where wellingtons belong

Ian, the Incredible Grumpy Hulk

I was on my way to the kitchen
To fetch myself a beer
When all of a sudden
From out of nowhere
The wife suddenly appeared
Charging through the door she came
Full steam ahead
Crash, bang, wallop, we collided
Head to head

Snacks and wine all over the floor
But worst of all
I stubbed and skinned my toe
On the bottom of the assailing kitchen door
The wife she said in an uncaring tone,
"What were you doing
Lurking behind the door anyway?
Don't you blame me,
It's your own silly fault"

I went from nought to murder in half a second
"Blooming, flipping heck," I cried
'Cause it didn't half bloody hurt
I clenched my teeth
As I pulled off my sock
I was turning green

As I blew my top
I closed my eyes
I couldn't bear to look
I'd split my toenail
Yes, there was blood

Growing on the end of my footsie
Was a purple pulsating blister
Like a volcano, it was growing
And ready to erupt
I had to anesthetise myself
With a couple more beers
Before the raging Hulk inside of me
Finally calmed down
And the pain dulled and disappeared

Yes, that was the Saturday night
My blood pressure shot up
And my eyes turned yellow,
Like David Banner,
And my wife declared that I was Ian
The potty-mouthed whinger
Otherwise known as
The Incredible Grumpy Hulk

Where's My Hat?

"If you tell me what you're looking for
I might be able to help"
I muttered something under my breath
"Okay," said the wife, "I won't"
I had turned the whole place upside down
Like a whirlwind passing through
I'd seen it, had it, kept it safe
Yet was clueless to where I'd put it

I swear I had it in my hand
And I placed it on the chair
I know I did, I'm sure I did
But my hat it wasn't there
For heaven's sake, where is my hat?
I was beginning to get quite cross
Sod it, I thought, I haven't the time
The shabby old rag can stay lost

My missus then asked,
"Have you found that thing you were looking for?"
I said, "No, my love, I have not"
She asked, "Is it thermal, warm and woolly,
Black with a hint of red?"
"Yes," I said, to which she replied,
"Well, all the time you've been trying to find,
It's been on your blooming head,
You daft bugger"

CHAPTER 2

Don't You Laugh at
Your Misfortunate Wife

Tears in Derbyshire

We'd had a lovely family day out
In Matlock Bath, Derbyshire
When the wife suddenly said,
"Let's take the cable car to the Heights of Abraham"
So, the wife and I, and the two dogs
Climbed aboard the cable car
For what was to be the last trip of the day

"Ooh, it's a bit high," she said
As the colour quickly drained from her cheeks
Then halfway across the cable car stopped
That's when she panicked and began to freak
The tears they flowed, so much so
She blew snot bubbles from out her nose
"I don't want to die, save us husband," she cried
Yes, it was my chance to be a superhero
On our ill-timed cable-car ride

I said, "If you remove your union-jack bra,
I could fasten the dog leads to the straps,
Thus attaching them to the belt loops of my jeans,
I could then parachute to the ground,
Just like James Bond.
Failing that, I could remove the belt from my trousers,
Loop it over the wires
And abseil down to the cable-car station below"

The wife said, whilst blowing her nose,
"You would do that for me?"
"Yes," I replied, "of course I would, my love,
Besides, it'll be dark soon and I wouldn't want
To miss my evening meal back at the B and B"
"You pig," she cried, "I thought you cared"
It was then that the cable car started moving again
"Hooray," I shouted,
"All safe now, we're nearly there"
Trouble was,
We still had the return journey to make

Mosquitoes in the Bedroom

As I climbed up wooden hill to bed
After completing my nightly chores
I could hear old wifey bashing about
Making one hell of a blooming noise
I poked my head around the door
She was jumping on the bed
The light shade was swinging from side to side
And her face was a bright shade of red

"What's with all the noise?" I asked
I thought she'd lost the plot
"There are mosquitoes in the bedroom," she replied,
"And it's your turn to give them a swat"
Well, some bright spark – the wife!
Had left the window open all evening
So all the mosquitoes from far and wide
Had congregated on our ceiling

She said, "I won't be able to sleep tonight,
Not until every last one has gone"
So I fetched my electric tennis-racket zappy thingy
And did battle until well after one
Well I zapped those beasties well and good
But my elbow was giving me grief
And soon I tired and lost my swing
And quite quickly I dropped off to sleep

When I opened my eyes
The first thing I saw
Were the splat marks all over the walls
The bedroom it reeked of singed fried bugs
Their corpses were stuck to the décor
There was an imprint of a slipper
On the ceiling next to the light
And the mosquitoes that were left
Had doubled in size
As they had eaten and were ready to fight

The missus had been bitten from head to toe
She retreated because of her wound
"I think I've got malaria," she whinged,
"I must have tasted better than you"
I had one weapon left in my arsenal
It was my very last line of defence
As dusk fell, I took up position
With my double-strength insect repellent

On the count of three
I stormed the bedroom
Giving those critters what for
One by one they fell at my feet
Their carcasses littered the floor
But the very next evening
As I finished up my chores
The missus shouts down to me,
"Husband, there are mosquitoes in the bedroom,
How am I supposed to sleep?"

My Moody-Moo

She whined and whinged, moaned and groaned
Then stormed off in a huff
"Your dinner's in the dog," she cried
And if that weren't bad enough
She lay there on the sofa
Wrapped up in the duvet
Four long hours of the silent treatment
That's what I got today

Yes, once a month for a couple of days
The wife she goes all wacko
Like Norman Bates in that horror flick
You know the one, *Psycho*
The dog and I we run and hide
Trying to avoid the flak
The trouble is, when we smell food
We both go running back

I don't know why she flipped her lid
But she threw an almighty strop
I received a tongue-lashing
Though I'm not quite sure for what
My Moody-Moo, I let her be
She was grouchy all day long
But by evening time I'd had enough
And asked, "Please tell me what is wrong"

She cried,
"My bum's too big,
I've put on weight,
I've got bingo wings and cankles,
I have facial hair, I'm getting old,
And my boobies have started to dangle,
My legs were thin, my hair was blonde,
I had not an ounce of fat,
Now I'm just a wrinkly witch,
With hair growing on my back"

"Is that all?" I bravely asked
She gave me a wifely stare
Her feet they stomped
The doors they banged
As she stormed her way up the stairs
Oh dear, I thought,
I've gone and done it now
I've upset the love of my life
Banished was I from the marital bed
It was the spare room for me again that night

Now to feel the wrath of an unhappy wife
Is more than a hubby can bear
The ill-tempered moods
The tantrums and strops
Sometimes, I do despair
But life's too short for falling out
We always make up in the end
For after all, she is my soulmate
And of course, my very, very best friend

Fake Tan, Burnt Bottom

Just thirty quick seconds
That's all it took
To get that bronzed-all-over look
Her lily-white ass turned beetroot red
She couldn't walk, or sit
She just lay on the bed

She cried,
"Please will you rub some camomile on,
But be gentle, 'cause it hurts"
So I rolled up my sleeves
Slapped on some cream
It was as much as my missus could bear

From where I lay
I gazed across
Her bottom was up in the air
There was a sunset in the bedroom
Radiation, I declare
I did not need a sidelight
To read my magazine
For the glow from off her butt cheeks
Lit up the room a treat

There were scorch marks on the ceiling
Her bum did sizzle and hiss

I feared my wife she may combust
And her bottom be burnt to a crisp
I could have grilled a couple of burgers
For her rump was about to catch fire
Though I thought it best to keep away
From those burning cheeks of desire

I told her,
"Next time you go to the tanning salon,
I suggest you keep your undies on,
'Cause with all-over tans,
Cometh pain and grief,
'Cause after all,
Beauty is only skin deep"

Crank Calls and Silly Texts

I think my wife's addicted
To her Samsung Galaxy 6
She takes it everywhere she goes
And checks it every minute
Her phone's become her lifeline
She takes it in the bath
But when she dropped it down the loo
I didn't half blooming laugh

Well, that got me in trouble
My number she deleted
At least she won't be texting me
When I'm only up the stairs
She speaks another language
It's called predictive text
Her fingers move so blooming quick
My eyes become perplexed

When I'm crashed out on the sofa
Covered in biscuit crumbs and dribble
Half asleep and catching flies
She thinks it'll be a giggle
To post a photo to the nation
Of my embarrassing situation
She don't care that I looked foolish
'Cause it got one hundred likes

Yes, crank calls and silly texts
Are non-stop every evening
If she can't interact with all her friends
Then life is not worth living
Yes, every day it beeps and pings
Her obsession never stops
For goodness sake,
Mrs Mobile, give it a rest
And turn the bloody thing off

Thank you

When the Wife Burnt the Soup

The wife's been in the kitchen again
To warm up a bowl of soup
She turned on the electric oven
And turned the ring to maximum heat
Before retiring to the front room
To text her friends
Before proceeding to fall asleep

It's a good job I came home when I did
Because the kitchen stunk like a blacksmith's forge
Her tomato soup had erupted
Hitting the ceiling
Peppering the dog
Splashing the walls
It had exploded all over the floor
What was left was burnt in the pan

It was then that the smoke alarm kicked in
"Oh my God," yelled the wife
As she quickly ran into the kitchen
"I forgot all about the soup," she said
Adding, "Don't you frown at me, husband,
It's just a culinary mistake,
Besides, I'm glad you're now home

'Cause you can prepare us
A scrummy cheese-and-tomato pasta bake"

And with that she simply disappeared
Leaving me to clean up her mess
Seemed a bit harsh

CHAPTER 3

The Troublesome Twosome Have Been in the Pub Again

My Big Belly

I pulled on my jeans last Saturday night
They wouldn't fit over my waist
I shrieked with grief and in disbelief
I gurned a displeasing face
I took a deep breath, sucked in my chest
I was huffing and puffing and blowing
I don't know how but I squeezed it all in
But was self-conscious of how it was showing

The wife she shouted in an impatient tone,
"Husband, are you ready?"
I said, "No, my love,
I'm having issues with my ever-increasing belly"
I was lacing my boots, but I could not bend
My stomach obscured my feet
"Hurry on up," the missus did whinge,
"I'm hungry and want something to eat"

At the Fox and Hounds
I ordered our grub
I had gamekeeper's pie and chips
The wife had risotto and we both had dessert
Before choosing to stay for the quiz
She hadn't drunk much but tipsy she was
Drinking one wine, one Pernod and black
When she bellowed out loud

So as all could hear,
"Husband, you look pregnant and positively fat"

She fell about laughing
And the whole pub gawped
I was stunned by my wife's remark
I was stuffed to bursting
And with lager fermenting
I couldn't help but let out a big burp
Saving my blushes, I quickly joked,
"Better out than in"
But my troubles had just begun

As I tried to save face
My jean button popped
Going off like a loaded gun
It left my jeans at lightning speed
Hitting the landlord in his left eye
They carted him off in an ambulance
His wife, she didn't half cry

In our village he is now known
As one-eyed Jack
The landlord at the Fox and Hounds
The magistrate gave me community service
And suggested I shed a few pounds

My wife she declared, "It's salads for you
With cress yoghurt for your pudding"
I cringed at the thought of no chips for tea
Not to mention the exercise
The walking, cycling and running

My stomach it felt like my throat had been cut
But at least my jeans now fit over my waist
But I still dare not go for a pint in the pub
No, the landlord I still cannot face

Drunk in Charge of a Bicycle

When we moved from the town to the country
It was a chance for us to get fit
But riding a bike gave me cramp in my legs
And my buttocks did ache quite a bit
To shed a few pounds and to lose my belly
The concept did fill me with hope
And over the summer we both toned up
Much fitter we certainly felt

Well it started quite well but temptation was rife
As each village did have its own pub
On our way past, we'd stop for a glass
As it was sure to do us some good
After a couple or three, last orders it be,
Tipsy we certainly were
It's hard to keep pedalling
When you can't stop swerving
Though most of the evening's a blur

Then, out of the blue,
My missus yelled out,
"Do you want to see something rude?"
She then pulled up her top
And out did pop, her wibbly-wobbly boobs
In utter surprise, I lost my stride,
My foot fell off the pedal

I veered to the right and off the road
Straight into a bunch of nettles

My spouse she laughed
As I picked myself up
My face all blotchy and blistered
It was then she declared
With a face bright red,
"You've made me wet my knickers"

Now saddle-sore and nettle-stung
My patience was wearing thin
My jeans were chafing around my bits
It was hard to crack a grin
Well, the wife and I were stiff for a week
The hangover had left us queasy
"No pain, no gain," the wife proclaimed
Well, I didn't expect it to be easy
Then came winter bringing wind and snow
Our flirt with fitness did end
And from that day on, I must confess
We've not been cycling again

When Bigfoot Crashed My Barbeque

Chillaxing in the garden with an ice-cold beer
When someone crept up behind me
And flicked me on the ear
I jumped up out my seat and yelled,
"You seven-foot hairy monster,
What do you think you're doing?"
And the stinky, hairy, flea-bitten beast
Pointed at the barbeque and asked,
"Any food going?"

He helped himself to sausages and burgers
And downed a six pack of beer
Before wandering back off into the brush
Where he simply disappeared
That's when the wife came home

Oh dear,
She gave me a wifely stare and asked,
"Where's the burgers, where's the buns?
Have you drunk all the beer?"
I said, "No, it was Bigfoot from the woods,
He came into the garden
Sat where you are
And proceeded to scoff and guzzle the lot"

The wife she didn't believe me
She told me I was selfish and greedy
Before storming off in a strop
Maybe I just dreamt all of this
Or maybe I was drunk
You decide, I'll leave that up to you
But one thing's for sure
On that August bank holiday Monday
I swear Bigfoot crashed my barbeque

Mrs Smith's Bloomers

"Blooming heck," I said to the wife,
"Come and have a look at these"
Blowing in the wind, drying in the sun
Was the world's biggest pair of briefs
The knickers on the line were
Forty times the size of mine
Sexy, they most certainly were not
Best parachute silk they might have been
But the thought of them being worn was a shock

Now Mrs Smith's bloomers at number eight
Were legendary in our village
For in the big flood of '89
They held back the tide, preventing a spillage
They had even been used as a windsock
By the local flying club
And when a hurricane hit,
Disaster was prevented
As they had patched up the roof of the pub

Each July at the village fete
Her bloomers were used as the marquee
In it there was room for
Ten adults, four kids, two dogs,
One pram and even an OAP
The main attraction at last year's event

Was the infamous bungee jump
But the elastic from her drawers
Was far too long
And so, one poor kid, didn't half go with a bump

It was then that a gust of wind detached her pants
Freeing them from their tether
They landed on my greenhouse roof
"Well," I said, "I never"
Now me and the missus we'd had a drink
We were in the mood for some fun
So we tied Mrs Smith's knickers
To our wheelie bin
And floated on up to the sun

High above the village we climbed
We could see Mrs Smith below
Waving, shouting, causing a scene
"Bring back my knickers," she did holler
Well, it wasn't easy balancing in a wheelie bin
We got snagged on St Peter's steeple
Downwards we plunged, with a tear in the gusset
Crashing amongst the people

Mrs Smith gave us a right good telling off
We'd trashed her luxurious undies
She cried, "If truth be told,
They were my favourite pair,
And I wore them for church on a Sunday"

My neighbour said they were custom-made
And had come with a matching bra
My eyes popped out
When I saw the size of the cup
However, it would have certainly
Kept the frost off your car

We apologised profusely
Though it didn't half cost me a fortune
To replace the extra, extra, extra-large set of lingerie
And no, there will be no more hot-air ballooning

Thank you

Playing Hangman with Albert Pierrepoint

Standing at the bar in the Anchor and Hope
When in walked this fella
Clenching three yards of rope
He pulled out a stool
Threw the rope around the rafters
He then tied a noose
As he chuckled with laughter

The landlord declared,
"Don't look him in the eye"
But I didn't get the chance to ask him why
'Cause he tapped me on the shoulder
He said, "Evening friend"
Then the landlord whispered,
"That's Albert Pierrepoint and you've been condemned"

He was the state executioner
The hangman champion
Who vowed to stretch my neck
And leave me dangling
Yes, I'd been challenged by the hangman king
To a paper-and-pencil guessing game
Now let the contest begin

Albert said, "Heads or tails to who goes first,
And best of luck this evening"
The landlady brought me
Steak pie and chips
And uttered, "Enjoy your last meal,
'Cause Albert's never been beaten"

It didn't fill me with confidence
I was trembling with fear
'Cause every time I guessed a letter wrong
Old Albert grinned from ear to ear
I knew I had to guess it right
It was on the tip of my tongue
I was one step away from losing
I couldn't afford to get it wrong

Tied it was at two games each
This was the decider
One word, nine letters, no clues
I was none the blooming wiser
But under pressure Albert succumbed
He'd included too many vowels
A fatal mistake, my chance I did take
Though I kept it close to my chest, for now

After I'd guessed the I and E, I asked,
"Is there an R in your word?
And is the last letter a D?"
Albert looked me in the eye
For he knew that he'd been beaten
I yelled out loud, "Reprieved"
Yes, that was the word that saved my soul
From swinging from the ceiling

I won't forget that look on Albert's face
His jaw dropped, his lip quivered
Then he shook my hand, untied his noose
And off he quickly slithered
Well, you won't see me in that pub again
For I'll never frequent that joint
'Cause I'll never forget that evening
Playing hangman with Albert Pierrepoint

HANGMAN

A B C D E̷ F G̷ H I J K L̷ M̷ N
O P Q̷ R̷ S̷ T U V̷ W̷ X H̷ Z

<u>G</u> _ <u>M</u> <u>E</u>

The Milkman, the Russian
and the Beast from the East

It was a bleak winter's night
Not fit for man nor beast
The village was cut off
The power was out
Imprisoned we were by an arctic blast
Which they had nicknamed
The Beast from the East

Most of the village had gathered at the pub
Where there was light, warmth
And plenty of beer and free grub
The wind was bitter and the snow was thick
When a policeman came in and asked,
"Has anyone seen the milkman?
His van's been found stuck in a snowdrift"

Now, Terry the milkman
Had started his round early
So as not to let anybody down
But the roads were blocked
And his van had got stuck
And as a result
He'd broken down

They found footprints in the snow
Which led across the field, to a barn
Where he'd gone to shelter from the cold
"Well, there you have it," voiced a farmer,
"He'll be safe in there, there's plenty of hay,
Yes, shut in a barn, with a hundred farting cows,
He'll be warm and dry and sedated by methane,
He'll be okay"

The landlord then quietly asked,
"Who's the stranger sat in the corner
In the fur coat and Cossack hat?"
Everybody stared but nobody knew
Then Beryl, the landlady, said,
"I don't know, he's not from around here
But he ordered a glass of vodka
And a large plate of my homemade stew"

The waitress asked Beryl,
"Should I go and ask him if he's alright?"
This she did
But as she got to his table
She found him slumped forward and lifeless
With that she screamed

"Is there a doctor in the pub?
'Cause this man appears to be dead"

A local farmer declared,
"He looks Russian
Maybe he's the spy that came in from the cold
Maybe he died of novichok poisoning
Or Beryl's warmed-up stew"

It was then that the doctor returned
After helping to rescue Terry
"I'll take a look and make a diagnosis," he said
"Well," said Beryl, "what's your verdict?"
The doctor then announced to the pub,
"There's no need to panic
This man did not die of poisoning
Nor Beryl's warmed-up stew
He died of hypothermia"

Beryl breathed a sigh of relief
And the stranger was taken away
Now every year on a cold winter's eve
The landlord and his wife
They love to tell the tale
Of the milkman, the Russian
And the Beast from the East

The man's identity
Remains a mystery to this very day

CHAPTER 4

There's Some Strange Goings-on in Our Village

Padre Pete the Flatulent Priest

I'm sorry to say but today was a sad day in our village
For it was Padre Pete's funeral
Now, me being the local gravedigger
I thought I'd go to church
And pay my respects
'Cause after all, he was a nice old chap
Despite his acute flatulence

Sat in the pew in front of me
Were two gossiping old women
I couldn't help but overhear
As the two women reminisced
About the padre and his wife

One of them said,
"I used to be her housekeeper, you know,
She didn't half enjoy her sherry
Morning, noon and night, allegedly
That's why she was always blotto and merry
She even had sherry on her cornflakes
Yes, she loved her drink
That's why on a Sunday morning
The church bells often rang out of sync"

Not to be out-beaten
The other lady then said,

"And what about Padre Pete himself
The flatulent priest
The phantom farter of the village
And his abrupt departure
After the marriage of Lord Snooty's daughter"

Oh yes, I remembered this,
That was the day that
Lord Snooty's daughter was getting married
My wife was her very best mate
So of course we both were invited
Conducting the day's proceeding
Was Padre Peter Kirtley
It was to be his last official engagement
As it would end in controversy

As the couple stood to take their vows
The Padre let out a fart
The raspberry ripple bellowed out loud
But this was just the start
The kids at the front they giggled and laughed
The bride-to-be she fainted
Her mother she cried
The groom dropped the ring
Her father was devastated

"I'm sorry," said Pete
As he broke wind again
Before climbing into his pulpit
"Well, I never," said the wife,
"I never had him down as the culprit"
"I apologise," said Pete,
"For I have ruined this couple's special day
From tomorrow
I will respectfully resign my post
And the wife and I will move away"

And yes, with immediate effect
Pete and his wife retired
They cleaned out the vicarage
And were gone in a flash
And from that day to this
They never looked back

Rest in peace Padre Pete
The Flatulent Priest
The Phantom Farter of the village

Billy the Catapult Kid

"I bet you can't hit the cockerel
On top of the church tower,"
Said Billy's younger sister Louise
"Of course I can," said Billy,
"You just watch me
I'll knock it off its perch, with ease"
He then pulled from his pocket a catapult
And with a marble used as ammo
He drew back the elastic as far as he could
And on three – he let go

The projectile hit the brass cockerel
Sending it whirling, around and around
"Told you I could do it," said Billy,
"Now give me my pound"
His mother had confiscated his catapult
After Billy had shot his own brother
But with money made from all those dares
He defiantly bought another

"I dare you to take out that street light,"
Said Billy's best buddy, Caine
"I could do it with one eye closed," said Billy,
"And if I do, you can give me all your loose change"
With his left eye closed Billy let fly

Smashing to smithereens the light
"Bullseye," yelled Billy out loud
As he and his mate took flight

"I bet you daren't catapult the postman,"
Said Josie, his sister's friend and accomplice
"Shoot him on the butt cheeks," she said,
"And if you do, I'll give you a big fat kiss"
But as Billy took aim and was about to launch
A policeman shouted, "Don't do it, son"
With that, Billy panicked and misfired his shot
Striking himself hard on the thumb

The constable grabbed him by the ear
And dragged him up the street
"I'll let your mother deal with you," he said
As Billy cried and shrieked
His thumb swelled up to four times its normal size
His fingernail dropped off
Yes, for poor old Billy the end was nigh
For Billy, he himself had been shot

Big John's Sofa

My neighbour, big John,
Weighs a whopping eighteen stone, 115 kilos
He's a self-confessed couch potato
Who's addicted to cheesy Doritos
His wife refers to him
As a good-for-nothing lazy slob
'Cause he spends most of his life
Festering on the sofa
Chilling out, watching Netflix, playing PS4
Just sat there with his very smelly dog

Now John's not the most agile of chaps
He doesn't do exercise
But when the springs on his sofa went pop
And pierced his backside
He soon jumped up
Letting out a shrieking scream
His wife, she laughed uncontrollably
So much so, she spat out her false teeth
She said, "You know what this means, John?
A new three-piece suite"

Now they were the words
That John did not want to hear
But his sofa had seen better days
His wife had always been too ashamed

To have guests over
Too embarrassed she was
To let anyone sit on John's toxic sofa
For it sagged in the middle
It was worn out and threadbare
Totally unhygienic, smelly
And covered in dog hair

With no further ado
Me and a friend dragged it outside
The shabby old thing,
It weighed as much as John
And it looked even worse in the daylight
My mate whispered,
"I wonder what rubbish has collected down the back,
Shall we have a look?"
"Good idea," I said,
"I'll fetch a face mask and some protective gloves"

Rummaging down the back
We promptly discovered
One half-eaten very sticky sherbet lemon
With fluff on it,
Muffin wrappers, pizza crust,
A mummified apple core,

A takeout menu,
A handful of chocolate Weetos,
Popcorn and a stinky sock
And a plentiful supply of cheesy Doritos
And, of course,
The obligatory one-pound coin

That's what we found down the back
Of Big John's sofa
And yes, your wife is right
Big John, it's official, you are a slob
You lazy loafer

Psycho Sam the Postie-Killer

Postman killer, Psycho Sam,
The recluse from number nine
Who never received a birthday card, nor a valentine
All he got were bills and junk
It used to drive him crazy
So he'd chase the postman up the street
Waving a rusty old machete

Lurking beside his letterbox
He conjured up a plan
Yes, our reckless neighbour from up the street
Would assassinate the postman
So when he called at half past ten
Delivering him a letter
In cold blood he stabbed him once
With a pointed umbrella

In the bath he chopped him up
He hid him in the freezer
He sliced and diced
With an electric saw
Into tiny little pieces
In the farmer's field up the lane
He fed him to the pigs
He thought he'd gotten away with it
Until one day, he got nicked

The judge, he said to Sam,
"You can't go around killing postmen"
And sent him off to gaol
Now he lives at Her Majesty's pleasure
Where he doesn't get any mail
Now Mr Sam
Lives mortgage free
Not one utility charge
'Cause now he has no bills to pay
The lucky bas-tard

Whiffy Wilf's Stinking Socks

I said to the wife,
"What is that terrible rancid stench?
It don't half blooming stink"
For days it had been drifting around the village
Though it's worse here on the High Street
It's not the farmer's muck heap
Or the slurry on his fields
It's not the drains, of that I'm sure
It's something more horrid, I feel

The village hall was packed that evening
As an emergency meeting was called
The missus and I
We stood and listened
As the chairman addressed us all
He said, "I have received many complaints,
From far and wide, regarding the lingering whiff,
So I've called in the Environmental Agency,
They'll get to the bottom of this"

Well, two men came, wearing protective suits
Holding smell-o-meters in their hands
Around and around the village they roamed
But still they drew a blank
Then all of a sudden

They beeped and bleeped
Their whiff-o-meters fused and fried
The pollution was coming from Watermill Farm
Where the readings were dangerously high

Stood in the yard was Wilf's dear wife
She'd been pleading for help for weeks
She declared, "I'm far too old,
To be chasing my hubby's socks,
Never mind washing his festering feet"
The stench was too much, even for Wilf
Who'd been sleeping with his feet
Out of the window
The result of which was a toxic cloud
Giving off a fluorescent glow

His farm was declared a no-go zone
They were trapped and in fear of his socks
A constable shouted over the wall,
"Don't worry, Wilf, we'll have you out of there
By eight o'clock"
Now Mr Wilf was served a summons
He was told to clean up his act
Most of his socks were incinerated
Though there were some
they just could not catch

His wellies, his boots, and even his feet
Were thoroughly disinfected and cleaned
And Wilf kept to his promise
And splashed out his cash
On a brand-new washing machine
His wife she grinned from ear to ear
She said, "My life is so much better"
And her hubby,
He vowed he'd bathe every day
And to spray his feet with a freshener

It was good to be able to sit out again
Free from the whiff of Wilf's feet
Where the only odour wafting around
Was the barbeques on the street
Who'd have thought that a few pairs of cheesy socks
Could cause such a potent pong
Though, come to think of it,
Mine aren't much better
Especially when I've had my work boots on

Twelve-Bore Pete

His wife she declared,
"You're not sitting in the house all day,
Getting under my feet,
Get yourself a hobby, or a dog"
So Pete went out and bought
Larry, a pedigree spaniel
Before accepting the position of gamekeeper
In the grounds of Lord Snooty's private lodge

"You've done what," yelled his wife,
"You've never set a snare, gutted a rabbit,
Or looked after grouse in your life"
"I know what I'm doing," replied Pete,
"Besides, how hard can it be?"
"OK," said his wife,
"On your head be it, but don't come crying to me"

As Pete had already been hired
He thought he'd get himself properly attired
A deerstalker hat, with shotgun and boots
A proper English gent
In his tweed fitting suit

Well, the villagers nicknamed him
Twelve-Bore Pete

'Cause his gun was as big as a cannon
They mocked,
"If he lets rip, it'll knock him for six,
And the blast will be heard
From here down to Devon"

From day one it didn't go well
The rabbits run amuck in the vegetable patch
The fox killed all the chickens
The woodland caught fire and burnt to a crisp
And the trout in the pond went missing

Then one dark night poachers came
Grouse and deer were shot
Pete was called to track down the toerags
But unfortunately, he got lost
Then Larry, his trusted hound,
Picked up their scent
And through brambles and bracken they trudged
In hot pursuit, they tracked them down
To a clearing at the edge of the woods

However, the poachers had spotted old Pete
And fled before he could catch up
But as Pete gave chase

He tripped on a log
Thus shooting himself in the foot

It was six months before Pete could walk again
He was then summoned up to the lodge
"I think we're going to get the sack," said Pete to Larry
But oddly, he got a promotion instead
Lord Snooty declared,
"You're not cut out to be a gamekeeper,
Though you couldn't have tried any harder,
I would like you to nurture my prize-winning
chrysanths,
Will you be my head gardener?"

The Lord had been county champion
For nine years in a row
Boasting, he said,
"This year I will be ten times titleholder"
How his little face did glow
What's a chrysanth? thought Pete
Besides, how hard can it be?
And without further ado,
He said to Lord Snooty,
"Yes, I'll take the job, you can certainly rely on me"

Whoops!

CHAPTER 5

Why Are You Grinning like a Cider-Fuelled Idiot?

Struck by Lightning

The day I got struck by lightning
Is a day I've never forgot
Frazzled was I by a mega bolt of electricity
Which incinerated me on the spot
I swear it gave me superhuman powers
'Cause my body felt revitalised
Yes, when I came to in the wet muddy field
I felt invincible and re-energised

Well, it all started when
I took the dog up the top field
It was a lovely summer's day
Then the sky it turned the colour of slate
A storm was on its way
Through darkened skies lightning flashed
In fear, I dived beneath a tree
Not a very clever move, I'm thinking to myself,
As the rain fell heavily on me

The dog was cowering by my side
But in fright he then took flight
It was then that I was paralysed
By a bolt of white light
In a flash my life did pass
My eyebrows were singed and scorched

My hair was gone
My ears smoked
And I dribbled when I talked

I staggered home looking like a zombie
My clothes all tattered and torn
My fingertips were blackened
My toes were glowing and warm
"Ooh, I bet that smarts," said the wife
No sympathy for me
I said, "That's no way to talk to a superhero"
But she just grinned and said,
"Shut up and drink your tea"

My missus dismissed my superhuman capabilities
Maintaining I was just a normal bloke
I said, "I can't save the world without a costume,
Will you knit me a cloak?"
"Don't be silly," she said
To which I replied,
"I am storm terror, lightning man,
My mission is to save the earth"
"You're not zooming off anywhere," she said,
"You've got your chores to do first"

Challenging her, I joked,
"I could click my fingers, create a spark,
Zapping you to a crisp"
"Go on, I dare you," she replied
Squaring up to me with her fists

But soon my powers began to fade
I became weak, run down and drained
And in order to retain my special powers
I would need to be struck down again
Well, I could not endure being zapped again
Not another lightning strike
So I had a bath and climbed into bed
And by morning I felt alright

Mr McNeal's Secret Pies

McNeal's butchers and bakery
Was a family-run business
That had been trading for over eighty years
Renowned they were, envied by some
For their award-winning pies and pastries
The recipes were a secret
Only known to one man
Though he promised his wife
Giving her his word
They'd be passed on to his eldest son

In this year's category in the 2011
Village pie championship
The challenge was
Who could bake the hottest,
Most tonsil-burning, lip-tingling
Fiery pie of them all

A rival in the neighbouring village
Had never beaten the McNeals
And so desperate was he
To win that trophy
That he had his two sons
Break in to the bakery

Hot out of the oven
Were half-a-dozen
Three-inch pies, resting on a cooling rack
They had located what they were looking for
The all-important experimental batch

Beside them was the packaging
This read:
"When eaten, drink plenty of water,
Do not kiss the wife,
Harmful and upsetting,
Do not consume if pregnant,
May cause flatulence and excessive sweating"

It was then that the alarm went off
Though it did not thwart their plan
They stole the pies and legged it
Speeding off in their cronky old van
Unwisely, they thought it best to eat the evidence
So they consumed the entire batch
When the police finally caught up with them
They were both found comatose in the back

A paramedic yelled,
"Open up the pharmacy,

I need two drips setting up with a litre
Of Gaviscon in each,
I need antacid tabs and Imodium,
And as a precaution,
You'd best clear the street"

Well, old man McNeal
Had predicted a break-in
But he could not have stopped production
So the pies he baked
Were a hoax indeed
And not fit for human consumption
He grinned and declared,
"That'll teach the thieving toerags,
No, they won't do that again,
Yes, my secret blend of spices and chillies
Will have them farting all weekend"

The two men were later discharged from hospital
And despite their father's pleas
Never again did they try to steal
The secret recipe from the McNeals

Bodge-It and Scarper Ltd

The wife and I we did decide
We finally made a decision
To completely gut the bathroom
And to extend the kitchen
So we called in all the tradesmen
To give us their usual quote
We vowed we would choose wisely
And Barney Bodge-It got our vote

On a Monday morning he arrived
My wife she wasn't impressed
"Who is that bogeyed builder?" she asked,
Somewhat distressed
I said, "It's Bodge-It and Scarper Ltd,
Established in '83,
A professional builder at an honest price,
And he estimates for free"

"Morning guv," said Barney,
"Now where would you like me to start?"
"I don't," said the wife in a deep stern voice,
"I've had a change of heart"
I took a deep breath and let out a sigh
For which I got a wifely stare
"I do not trust him; he'll get it wrong,

He's incompetent,"
My wife declared

He had a plaster on each of his fingers
And a drill hole in his hand
A bandage on his forehead
And tea stains all over our plans
No, he did not fill us with confidence
Of that I must declare
Though there was something about his sales pitch
That had already made us aware

His advert it read:
"No job too big, no task too small
Barney Bodge-It is your man
I've all the gear but no idea;
I've even got a van
I do put off till tomorrow,
What I could do today
So, pick up the phone, call Barney
And I'll get back to you, sometime, someday"

Well, for Barney Bodge-It Ltd
Established in '83
We gave him the boot I'm afraid
Despite him reducing the fee
"No," screamed the wife,
"I would like you to leave"
And he tore our quote in half
And as a parting gesture
He pulled us a moon
Yes, he gave us the full builder's ARSE

Eight-Legged Fred

When the spider came in from the cold
He crept in through the window
He crawled across the ceiling
Making our home, his home
He ate all the other spiders
And scared away the mouse
Even the dog gave up his bed
As the spider took over our house

I know he has to live somewhere
But come on, you're not wanted
You're not welcome here
But he wouldn't go
I think he'd settled in for the winter, so much so
That I offered him a slice of toast, and asked,
"Will you be staying for Christmas lunch?
'Cause if so, I'll buy you a gift"

I guess the front room was warmer
Than the outside shed
And as neither I nor the wife
Dared to evict him
We thought we'd give him a name instead
So quite fittingly
We named him Eight-Legged Fred

Now Fred spun a web
In the corner of the living room
Directly above the TV
And every time I'd fetch the remote
He'd wink his spidey eye at me
Yes, he'd watch my every move
And every time he trapped a fly
He'd dance the arachnid groove

But the next morning
When I came downstairs
I thought, *Yippee, he's gone*
I couldn't find Fred anywhere
But then I noticed another spider
A much bigger one
This one was ginormous
It must have been on steroids
'Cause his legs were twice the size of mine

I thought, *We can't keep going on like this*
So I decided to face him head-on
Besides, he must have eaten poor old Fred
I know it's survival of the fittest
But that's just wrong

With one quick swipe
I took him by surprise
I caught him in a jam jar
And released him outside
With a joyful goodbye
R-I-P Fred

Old Man's Nap

Sundays, they are boring
Especially in the winter
When I like to laze in front of a fire
In just my joggers and a jumper
Self-indulged on Sunday lunch
Lethargic and relaxed
Now I've reached the big five-o
I need an old man's nap

Yes, by half past two in the afternoon
My eyes are feeling heavy
It's grey and wet and cold outside
And Poirot's on the telly
I was on the brink of nodding off
Comfy in my chair
When the wife came in and yelled at me,
"Don't you bloody dare"

As I approach my twilight years
I've lost all motivation
I'm getting old, I'm slowing down
It's natural progression
Can't stop myself from yawning
My body needs recharging

Caught was I by the wife again
Who accuses me of snoring

Well, she stands need
She's younger than me
I often catch her sleeping
Lying on the sofa, catching flies
So early in the evening
I do admit I power-nap
Just to rest my eyes
And I've been told I dribble a bit
And it's not a very pleasant sight

What I need is exercise
Some fresh air in my lungs
But I can't be bothered to get out my chair
To do a 10K run
Don't like the thought of getting old
In fact it's pretty sad
'Cause now I've reached the big five-o
I need my old man's nap
Goodnight

KO'd by the Wife

It's fair to say that I don't sleep well
But when I do I dream
In some I'm quite heroic
Whilst others are just downright obscene
In one I had quite recently
I was boxing for the title
Yeah, Bruno and I
Face to face
With a crowd both jubilant and wild

The bell it rung and out I come
I was sure that I would win
But the next thing I know
I'm in row C
I'd took a right hook to my chin
I barely had a chance to raise my fists
When gone were all my hopes
The power within that whacking thump
Had launched me over the ropes

When I came around from my punishing bout
I was laid on the bedroom floor
Ooh I ached
I was in discomfort
But bizarrely, it was my ribs that were sore

Black and blue and ego-bruised
To my bed I crawled back in
It was then that the penny finally dropped
It was the wife who'd put the boot in

My spouse lay but a foot away
Chattering in her sleep
Dreaming in the land of nod
But kicking out with her feet
She yelled out loud,
"Kick on girl, kick on"
Lashing out like a mare possessed
I caught her mid karate
Pinning her legs to the mattress

I thought, *I've got to put a stop to this,*
As it can't go on no more
So, I gently eased her out of bed
And she tumbled on the floor
I said to her sarcastically,
"Oh dear, have you fallen from your horse?"
"Yes," she replied, "I must have done,
But did I finish the course?"

Now whenever the wife's playing horsey
Thus preparing for an event
The night before I cannot sleep
In fear of her excitement
So when I climb up wooden hill
And pull the duvet over my head
I hope she won't KO me
But will snuggle me instead

The Budgerigar's Revenge

The wife, she kept no secrets
She told it how it was
Then one day she let it slip
About the budgie and my breakfast
She laughed so much the tears they flowed
I could not comprehend
It seemed that I was unaware
Of the budgerigar's revenge

The budgie's name was Tekki
A spirited little soul
A cheeky chap with character
Fearless and quite bold
I must admit I was not too keen
He often freaked me out
His aerobatics were just too much
In our small suburban house

At breakfast time he'd swoop and dive
He'd zoom around the room
He pecked at all the furniture
Whilst whistling out a tune
One morning I was sat there
Chomping on my muesli
When Tekki flew across the room
And purposely dumped a doody

Myself, I did not see it
The wife however did
But she kept hush and did not tell
Of the budgie's well-aimed hit
In my bowl the doody did land
This mixed in nicely with my bran
Heaped on my spoon, I did not see
Down the hatch, *Mmm, yummy*

It was only after the budgie had died
That I found out what he'd done
He'd swooped and pooped
And I had chewed
Yes, I'd swallowed it down in one
I guess he got me well and good
Though worse was yet to follow
'Cause Roger and Gerald
The parrots from hell
Are coming to live with us tomorrow

CHAPTER 6

More Tomfoolery at Shipley Towers

Sprouting Nose Hairs

Went to sleep one evening
Woke up the next morning
With nose hairs protruding
Sprouting from my nostrils
Germinating overnight
Propagating in my nasal cavity
Emerging at first light

Nostrils with extending tufts
Bursting from my snout
Where the blooming hell did they come from?
And no, I'm not pulling them out

I looked in the mirror
They were hideously long
I had to snip them with wire cutters
Because they were that thick and strong

It's the same with my eyebrows
And my ears
It must be an old-man thing
Whiskers flourishing everywhere
Well, that's all well and good
But why, oh why
Won't hair grow on my head?

The Sausage-Thieving Labrador

Last Wednesday evening
I made the mistake
Of leaving two defenceless
Lincolnshire pork and Bramley apple sausages
Resting on my plate
I'd only walked across the kitchen
To fetch myself some bread
But when I returned to the table
I found instead

Dog slobber on the carpet
Dog slobber on the chair
Dog slobber in my shoe
Dog slobbers were everywhere

The sausages were gone
And so was the dog
I followed the gravy trail
Which led to his bed
There he sat looking pleased and content
Wagging his tail
I knew what that meant

He gave me his paw
Yes, he was guilty for sure

A sausage thief
A law-breaking canine
At least now he doesn't need feeding
And with that
He curled up in his basket
Where he settled down for the evening

The thief!

Chippy-Chip Thursday

There was a notice in our village magazine, it read,
"From next month on a Thursday evening,
Between 7pm and 9,
A chip van will park outside the church,
Please form an orderly line"

Sitting in my comfy chair
I yelled out loud, "Hooray"
I was drooling at the thought of chips for tea,
And thinking, *I hope they do onion rings,*
To dip in my curry sauce

My spouse invited all the jodhpur girls
From the stables she was at
So Thursday night was proclaimed chip night
'Cause they all came around for fodder, tea
And a whinge and a chat

I was always happy to do the chip run
When the fillies wouldn't queue in the rain
Ooh, that wonderful smell of the chip van
Tantalising my taste buds
As I walked up the lane

Well, the girls weren't as piggish as me
They had cheesy chip cobs

I had large chips, a meat pie,
With onion rings and curry sauce
And there was always a freebie sausage for the dog

Ooh, I did enjoy my artery-clogging feast
Washed down with a cold can of pop
In fact we all enjoyed our fast-food treat
From the mobile fish-and-chip shop

But when winter arrived
The chip van never came
What's going on here, I thought
And a man walking his dog, he shouted across,
"The chip van isn't coming anymore"

No, Thursday evenings were never the same
'Cause those oven chips were bland and dry
What a shame,
'Cause I quite enjoy listening
To those gossipy horsey girls
It kind of made my night

Wife-Saver

With haste and greed
She munched through her food
Like piggy at the trough
Take your time
"I'm starving," she said
It was then that she began to cough
Her eyes they streamed
Her face turned red
The wife began to choke
She could not breathe
And began to wheeze
"I've got something stuck in my throat"

For a second I stood there quite helpless
Unsure of what I should do
"Are you OK?" I stupidly asked
As her lips began to turn blue
She was down on her knees
Gasping for air
I thought she was going to croak
"Fetch me a glass of water," she cried,
"I've got something stuck in my throat"

I put my arms around her waist
And pushed with a quick upward thrust
She belched and coughed

And out it flew
A chunk of wholemeal crust
I had saved the life of my dear wife
With some first-aid knowledge
She said,
"I'm grateful to you dear husband of mine,
Thank you for clearing my blockage"

Sexy-Rocker-Girl.com

"What are you looking at?" asked the wife
"Nothing," I said
"That means you're doing something
You shouldn't be doing," she replied
I was; I was looking at Sexy-Rocker-Girl.com
Which surprisingly had popped up on my Facebook page

Well, it would have been rude
Not to have taken a quick look
But the wife, she caught me
She blew her top,
Called me a perverted porno surfer
I said, "I'm not"
But she didn't believe me

It was the spare room for me again that night
All because of curvy, long-legged,
Punk, goth, rocker-chick photos,
Which remarkably appeared on my PC screen

So, if Sexy-Rocker-Girl.com
Pops up on your PC screen
Don't look
You'll get in trouble
I won't be doing this again, will I?
Honest!!!!

Specky-Four-Eyes (1978)

When I was a little boy
They used to call me names
I was Joe 90
In my National Health frames
They used to call me goggle-box
They used to call me gigs
They used to call me the Milky-Bar Kid

Yes, I was Specky-Four-Eyes
A nerdy little geek
A four-stone weakling
With lots of lip and cheek
I thought I looked like Michael Caine
In my black-rimmed specs
But I was Ronnie Corbett
In a Marks and Spencer vest

Yes, I was gogz
The four-eyed lad
A gawky little dweeb
A scrawny little so and so
A puny little weed
No, I wasn't Buddy Holly
Or Brains from *Thunderbirds*
Cause I was Specky-Four-Eyes
In a classroom full of nerds

CHAPTER 7

I'll Finish with the Last One

The Upturned Plug

It was as black as a hat
Around half past three
When an unforeseen mishap
Did happen to me
In the midst of the night
Thrown on the floor
Was a hairdryer plug
On which I did fall

Unseen in the darkness
Lurked the plug
Upturned and lethal
On it I stood
My eyes filled up,
I reeled in pain
Then a voice from beneath the duvet said,
"You won't do that again"

"No, my love," I said dismayed
From the three-pinned attack
An imprint was made
The solid brass pins
Had dug in my heel
I whimpered and whinged
Quite sick I did feel

In my distress, I fell on the bed
This woke the wife
Who quickly saw red
"What's with all the noise?"
My beloved did blurt
I shrieked, "I stood on a plug,
And it really did hurt"

"You should look where you are going,"
My loving spouse said,
"Now, go make a brew or come back to bed"
So, me and my foot we hobbled downstairs
I sat on the sofa,
My footsie I nursed

So please, heed my advice
Please be aware
That an upturned plug
Can cause pain and despair
No, nothing hurts more
Than those three-pinned killers
So don't go barefooted –
Wear your slippers

The End

CPSIA information can be obtained
at www.ICGtesting.com
Printed in the USA
LVHW110723120822
725756LV00004B/67

9 781803 811482